Durham County Council

Adults, Wellbeing and Health
Libraries, Learning and Culture

Please return or renew this item by the last date shown.
Fines will be charged if the book is kept after this date.
Thank you for using your library.

Renew online at www.durham.gov.uk/libraryonline

Daniel Green

HEALTHY DINING for Life

Marshall Cavendish Cuisine

Food photographs by Justin Grierson

Copyright © 2011 Marshall Cavendish International (Asia) Private Limited

Published by Marshall Cavendish Cuisine
An imprint of Marshall Cavendish International
1 New Industrial Road, Singapore 536196

National Library Board, Singapore Cataloguing-in-Publication Data

Green, Daniel,1970-
Healthy dining for life / Daniel Green. – Singapore : Marshall Cavendish Cuisine,
c2011.
p. cm.
Includes index.
ISBN : 978-981-261-640-1

1. Low-fat diet – Recipes. 2. Cooking. 3. Cookbooks. I. Title.

TX714
641.56384 -- dc22   OCN667454396

Printed in Singapore by KWF Printing Pte Ltd

To my best buddy for 25 years, Nicholas Rishover
This one's for you

"I was once obese. Through healthy eating, I lost 30 kg (65 lb) and have kept the fat off for 20 years. Give my recipes a try."

contents

have some tasty indulgences each day & still keep the weight off...

The first question people ask me when they see me is how I manage to come up with so many recipes. I travel a lot in the course of my work and on these trips, I discover new ingredients which I can draw inspiration from. Some of these new ingredients include sesame chilli oil, miso paste, udon noodles, black beans and dashi, which I will be using in the recipes in this book.

Although I live in America, my passion is for Asian food and this will always be apparent in my recipes.

This book will feature the dishes that I personally make and enjoy for my own daily meals from breakfast, lunch, dinner and snacks. It will include dishes that taste great and are really healthy, and which have helped me keep the weight off.

Some diets work because of the small portion sizes recommended for each meal. I have a big appetite, so such diets will not work for me as I will still be hungry. Instead, I eat large portions of my low fat food which keep me satisfied and trim! If you're looking to lose weight, I hope these recipes will provide you with the weight loss solution.

With love and thanks...

I am always trying out new ideas and new ways to cook. It's a passion that seems to only grow. This year I have filmed almost 100 episodes of *Kitchen Takeover*, a show where I go into people's homes without any idea what they have in the kitchen and help them cook a quick healthy dish in real time. I have posted many of the episodes on YouTube, with great thanks to my producer Sarah Rieland who also edits it to perfection.

I also am a presenter at ShopNBC. I am on 'live' five days a week and have been there almost six years. I love 'live' TV and it never feels like work. There was a time when I had no idea what I would do for work, and I did not dream I could love what I do for a living. I feel so blessed doing what I do. Thanks, everyone at ShopNBC.

This year I travelled to Singapore to film a series on the Li TV channel, had two books released by Marshall Cavendish International Asia, and hosted a successful event at the American Club in Hong Kong. I was also in Sydney on-air with TVSN. I can't thank my agent, business partner and friend, Vivien Lee, enough for helping me to set up these opportunities.

The biggest passion in my life remains my daughter, Eleanor and my wife, Jane. Thanks also to my mum and dad, in-laws Jennifer and Tony, and all my siblings for making me who I am today.

I hope you will make this cookbook a part of your everyday healthy eating regime and use it to prepare great tasting food for you and your loved ones.

Happy Cooking!

a food safety reminder from Daniel

Food passes through many hands before it arrives in our kitchens—and there is always the danger of contamination. As such, we should not forget the importance of sanitation in our home kitchen. Food safety should always be a priority, so please bear in mind these tips when preparing your next meal.

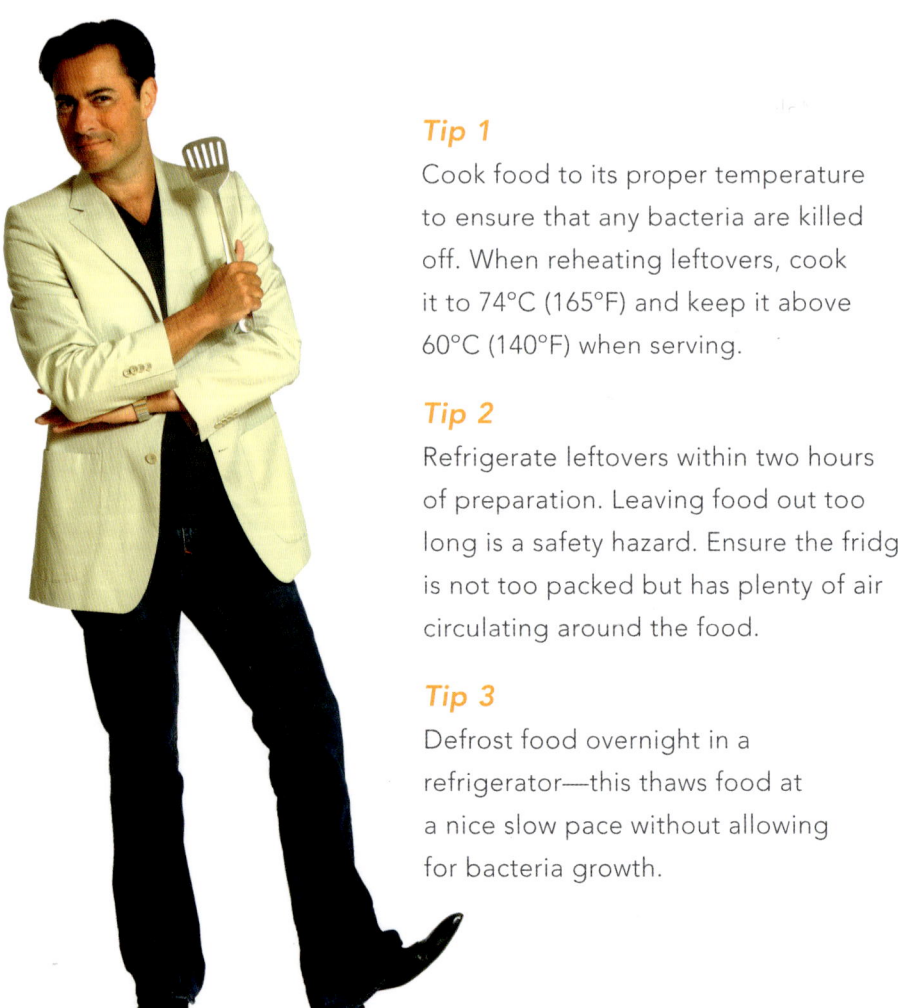

Tip 1

Cook food to its proper temperature to ensure that any bacteria are killed off. When reheating leftovers, cook it to 74°C (165°F) and keep it above 60°C (140°F) when serving.

Tip 2

Refrigerate leftovers within two hours of preparation. Leaving food out too long is a safety hazard. Ensure the fridge is not too packed but has plenty of air circulating around the food.

Tip 3

Defrost food overnight in a refrigerator—this thaws food at a nice slow pace without allowing for bacteria growth.

Tip 4

Always wash your hands well before you start any work in the kitchen. Also, wash everything you eat, even fish and meats, as they have been handled by many people.

Tip 5

Wash all fresh produce, even pre-packaged greens, to minimise potential bacterial contamination. Make sure kitchen counters, sponges, cutting boards and knives are all well-scrubbed. And don't use the same cutting board for both meat and vegetables.

Tip 6

Only freeze food for up to six months. Food that has been stored for longer will lose its taste and the texture will also deteriorate.

Tip 7

Don't let guests eat with their fingers or help themselves this way to food from communal serving—always put out serving utensils.

Tip 8

Never keep out-of-date or expired food, however much you spent on it.

Tip 9

Do not refreeze food more than once. Germs can flourish once food is thawed and the food will not be fresh the second time around.

Tip 10

Cold food should always be served at 5°C (40°F) or lower. Likewise, the temperature in your refrigerator should also be 5°C (40°F) or lower.

Green's Twist:
smart changes for healthier cooking & eating habits

As an advocate for healthy eating, people often ask me how they can lose weight. There are many kinds of diets that one can go on, and these may work for some, but for others, these diets may not be practical or sustainable.

Through my personal experience, I have found that making small changes over time will make big differences, and it will be something you can maintain without too much of a struggle. Here are some tips which I have personally found useful.

The recipes in this book also feature one or more tweaks which I call "Green's Twist" for a healthier approach to enjoying good food.

Daniel's activities in 2010 (from left): Co-hosting an episode of Bizarre Foods, for the Travel Channel in the US; creating and launching e-cookbooks for Président® Cheese (www.greatcheese.com/skinny); and in Sydney for The Big Olive culinary event.

Tips For Eating Out

Order a dish that is mainly made up of protein. Ask to substitute carbohydrates (such as potato, rice and pasta) with vegetables instead. Restaurants generally serve them in generous portions, so don't worry about going away hungry.

Choose your restaurant based on the cuisine they serve. For example, Japanese and Thai cuisines have a wide variety of healthy dishes.

Always ask for the dressing for your salad to be on the side. Restaurants tend to pile on creamy dressings such as Ranch and Caesar, which have high fat content. Alternatively, ask for vinaigrette or oil-based dressings instead.

Tips For Losing Weight

Forget fad diets; the best way to lose weight is to sustain a healthy diet. By cutting out food that is high in fat content, you'll have better and longer-lasting results.

Don't snack late at night; whatever food you may eat will be "wasted" energy. If you must, take fruit juice or yoghurt as a snack instead.

I do not agree with people who say "don't weigh yourself"; on the contrary, weighing yourself makes you more aware of how much physical activity you are doing, and what you eat every day.

Don't feel guilty about treating yourself a little during the weekend! As long as you eat a balanced diet and lead a healthy lifestyle, enjoy food for what it is!

Tips For Healthy Cooking

Try brushing your food with a little oil before cooking, instead of using oil to cook the food. Better yet, try cooking without oil. Invest in good-quality non-stick cookware which will minimise the need for oil. You'll be amazed at the results!

When cooking meats such as beef or lamb, place the meat over a bed of rock salt, then cook in the oven. The salt absorbs the fat from the meat but keeps it moist and juicy.

I've said it before, and I'll say it again: say no to deep-frying, cooking with butter, cream and cheese, on a daily basis!

breakfast

Low Fat Muffins 15

Low Fat Fry-Up 16

Olive Bread 18

Berry Blast 20

New Mango Smoothie 22

Feta Cheese Omelette 24

Low fat muffins offer a great start to any day, with carbs that release energy gradually.

low fat muffins

Serves 12

250 g (9 oz / 2 cups) plain (all-purpose) flour

165 g (6 oz / ³/₄ cup) sugar

1 tsp baking soda

1 tsp ground cinnamon

¹/₄ tsp ground nutmeg

1 large egg, lightly beaten

4 Tbsp extra virgin olive oil

250 ml (8 fl oz / 1 cup) nonfat milk

1 cup fresh cranberries

- Preheat oven to 180°C (350°F).
- Grease 12 muffin cups using a cooking spray (use a nonfat one if you can), or line with paper muffin cases.
- In a large bowl, mix flour, sugar, baking soda, cinnamon and nutmeg.
- Beat egg, extra virgin olive oil and milk in another bowl. Add the cranberries and flour mix. Gently fold with a wooden spoon or spatula.
- Spoon batter into muffin cups, filling them three quarters of the way. Bake for 20 minutes.

low fat fry-up

Serves 2

Everyone loves a great start to the day. As a child, my mum used to take me to a diner that had an all-day breakfast menu. We would always order the full breakfast or fry-up. Here is a healthier version.

1 potato, peeled

Extra virgin olive oil

4 white button mushrooms, halved

2 large tomatoes, halved

4 eggs

2 ham steaks, fat trimmed off
  (or use thinner slices of ham, if preferred)

1 can baked beans

- Slice the potatoes into chips or fries.
- In a nonstick pan, add a little extra virgin olive oil. Pan-fry potato chips or fries for about 4 minutes each side. Set aside.
- Reheat the pan and add the mushrooms Add the tomatoes face down and cook for a few minutes.
- Remove the mushroom and tomatoes, then fry the ham for a few minutes to heat it up. Remove from heat.
- Crack an egg into the pan and cook for 3–4 minutes or done to your preference. Repeat until eggs are done.
- Pour the baked beans into the pan to heat.
- Arrange on serving dishes and serve immediately.

olive bread

Serves 4

Making bread puts people off. I used to feel that way too, until I came up with this easy recipe. Try it!

250 ml (8 fl oz / 1 cup) warm water

1 Tbsp dried yeast

4 Tbsp extra virgin olive oil

3 Tbsp fresh rosemary, finely chopped

$^3/_4$ cup olives, pitted

375 g (13$^1/_4$ oz / 3 cups) plain (all-purpose) flour

- In a large mixing bowl, mix warm water and yeast stirring until it is well-mixed.
- Add the extra virgin olive oil, rosemary, olives and flour and mix well into a dough. Knead until smooth and cover with a damp cloth. Let sit for about 1$^1/_2$ hours until doubled in size.
- Shape dough into a large round.
- Preheat oven to 200°C (400°F), and bake for about 40 minutes.

berry blast

Serves 4

Made with four types of berries and ricotta cheese, this drink will provide you with the energy for a great start to the day!

1 cup blackberries

1 cup blueberries

1 cup strawberries

2 cups raspberries

4 cups fat-free ricotta cheese

$^1/_2$ cup sugar

Ice cubes

- Rinse berries well, then drain or pat dry with paper towels. Cut strawberries in half.
- In a blender, blend the ricotta and sugar. Add the berries and process. There should be enough juice in the berries to give this a smooth and thick consistency. If not, you can add a little orange juice or fat-free milk.
- Pour into serving glasses over ice and serve immediately.

new mango smoothie

Serves 4

The best mango smoothie I've tried is from a small stall in Chinatown in Kuala Lumpur, Malaysia. It makes a great breakfast drink.

2 ripe mangoes

1 banana, peeled

250 ml (8 fl oz / 1 cup) freshly squeezed orange juice

1 Tbsp grated ginger

Ice cubes

- Peel the mango and take off all the flesh. Place in a blender with the other ingredients and process until smooth.

- Pour into serving glasses over ice and serve immediately.

feta cheese omelette

Serves 2

Omelettes are actually quite tricky to make—we think of eggs as basic but that is not always the case. I pride myself on not only showing you the best way to make something healthy, but the easiest way to do it. Here is one such recipe.

Egg whites from 6 eggs

Extra virgin olive oil

$1/2$ white onion, peeled and finely sliced

6 mushrooms, sliced

1 cup fat-free feta cheese

- Place the egg whites in a bowl and set aside.
- In a pan, drizzle some extra virgin olive oil or use a cooking spray to coat the pan. Cook half the onion and half the mushrooms for 3–4 minutes. Then add half the cheese.
- Add in half the egg whites and swirl the pan to ensure egg whites evenly coat the base. Flip in half when cooked.
- Repeat for the next omelette.
- Serve immediately with a salad of choice.

appetisers

I love beluga caviar (see Note below), but I don't love the price. So I have developed a way to enjoy it—using much less expensive, but no less delicious orange roe.

poor man's caviar

Serves 4

2 eggs, hard-boiled
1 red onion, peeled
A handful of chives
60 g (2 oz) orange fish roe (salmon or trout)
4 slices of bread, toasted

- Peel the hard-boiled eggs and separate the whites from the yolks.
- Grate the egg whites and set aside, then do the same with the yolks.
- Chop the onion very fine and set aside. Do the same with the chives (I use scissors for the chives).
- Arrange egg white, yolk, fish roe, chives and onion on a plate and serve with toast.

Note:
Caviar is processed sturgeon roe—but in recent years, the sturgeon has been overfished in the Caspian Sea. This recipe uses fish roe from more sustainable food sources.

sticky spicy edamame

Serves 4

I create recipes with inspiration from my experience, and then add my Twist. This recipe was created after I tried the edamame at Tiger Sushi at the Mall of America in Minneapolis. This dish is amazing. Try it!

Cooking oil

700 g (1^1/$_2$ lb) edamame beans, in pods

4 Tbsp soy sauce

2 Tbsp water

1 Tbsp brown sugar

2 Tbsp sesame oil

3 bird's eye chillies, finely chopped

- Heat a large pan with a little oil. Add the edamame beans, then all the remaining ingredients. Stir well.
- Cook for a few minutes until sticky and serve.

tofu in mirin

Serves 4

I have grown to love tofu—the more delicate the flavour,
the better. This is a perfect dish, with a bit of mirin and
miso sauce.

700 g (1^1/$_2$ lb) spinach
Extra virgin olive oil
450 g (1 lb) medium tofu, sliced into
  2.5-cm (1-in) slices
2 Tbsp mirin
1 tsp miso paste
2 Tbsp white sesame seeds
2 Tbsp water

- Bring a pot of water to boil and blanch spinach to cook lightly.
  Remove and drain well. Keep warm.

- In a large nonstick pan, heat a drizzle of extra virgin olive oil
  and cook tofu on each side for 1 minute.

- Meanwhile, mix the mirin, miso paste, sesame seeds and water
  in a cup. Add to the pan, then take off the heat.

- Add the spinach and toss well.

- Serve the tofu with the spinach.

japanese oysters

Serves 4 to 6

I am not a fan to flavour oysters with vinegar or Tabasco.
So here is a much more delicate way to enjoy them.

2 tsp rice wine

1 tsp wasabi paste

1 tsp sesame oil

1 tsp light soy sauce

24 oysters on half shell

1–2 sheets of seaweed (nori), cut into strips

- Mix all the ingredients except the oysters and seaweed.

- Drizzle some dressing on top of each oyster.

- Garnish each oyster with some seaweed and serve immediately.

seared scallops on spinach

Serves 2

Scallops are so delicious when cooked right. Cook them over high heat quickly and never over-cook them. My friend Jimmy DeMunno gives mean competition for this one.

4 Tbsp extra virgin olive oil + more for pan-frying

1 clove garlic, peeled

A handful of fresh basil leaves

6 scallops

300 g (11 oz) spinach

2 shallots, peeled and chopped

- In a blender, add 4 Tbsp extra virgin olive oil, garlic and basil and process until blended. Set aside.

- Heat a little extra virgin olive oil in a large saucepan. Add the scallops and cook for 2 minutes on each side. Meanwhile, in another pan, add the spinach and a drizzle of extra virgin olive oil and heat until wilted.

- Add the shallots to the pan of scallops for the final minute of cooking time.

- Arrange scallops and spinach on serving plates and drizzle with garlic and basil dressing. Serve immediately.

the american club tuna tartare

Serves 4

I had something close to this at the American Club in Hong Kong. Chef Suzanne made us a lunch not to forget, and I had the privilege to enjoy it with great friends, Vivien and Layne.

450 g (1 lb) sashimi grade tuna

1 Tbsp white sesame seeds

1 tsp sesame oil

1 avocado, halved and peeled

Juice of $\frac{1}{2}$ lemon

2 tsp dashi powder

4 Tbsp hot water

1 tsp dried bonito flakes

- Chop the tuna into small cubes and mix in the sesame seeds and sesame oil. Set aside.

- Cube the avocado, squeeze over the lemon juice and set aside.

- Mix the dashi powder with the water and bonito flakes.

- Assemble the dish, avocado first, topped with the tuna and then drizzle over the stock.

- Spoon the avocado into individual serving plates and top with tuna. Drizzle with dashi stock.

swordfish tartare

Serves 4

In all my recipe books, I have always included my favourite fish tartare in some form or another. So here is my latest—swordfish tartare. I love how the flavours meld together here.

450 g (1 lb) fresh sashimi grade swordfish
$1/_2$ red onion, peeled
4 spring onions (scallions), finely chopped
$1/_2$ clove garlic, peeled and crushed
Juice of $1/_2$ lemon
1 Tbsp light soy sauce
A handful of fresh basil leaves, chopped

- Chop the swordfish into small cubes and set in a bowl.
- Chop the red onion the same way and add to the bowl.
- Add everything else and mix well. Serve immediately.

scallop ceviche

Serves 4

Raw fish is not just popular in Japan—many South American and African dishes feature raw fish too. Ceviche is a popular dish in South America, using raw seafood marinated with citrus juices. My version uses scallops and lime.

8 large sashimi grade scallops

Juice of $1/2$ lime

1 Tbsp extra virgin olive oil

A handful of chives, chopped

4 shallots, peeled and finely chopped

1 tsp rock salt

- Slice the scallops finely and place on a serving plate. Squeeze the lime juice over, then drizzle with extra virgin olive oil.

- Top with the chives and shallots and rock salt

- Serve immediately.

mediterranean stuffed squid

Serves 4

I once did a travel show in Spain, which gave me a great insight into Spanish food and inspired this recipe using squid, one of my favourite seafood items.

300 g (11 oz) salmon fillet
220 g ($^1/_2$ lb) peeled prawns
A handful of fresh basil leaves
1 tsp light soy sauce
$^1/_2$ red onion, peeled
4 large squid tubes or 8 smaller ones
1 Tbsp extra virgin olive oil
400 g (14$^1/_3$ oz) can of tomatoes
1 clove garlic, peeled and crushed
1 small chilli, chopped

- Place the salmon, prawns, basil, soy sauce and onion in a blender and process to a chunky mix.

- Stuff the mix into the squid tubes.

- Heat the extra virgin olive oil in a saucepan. Add the tomatoes, garlic and chilli and cook for 2 minutes.

- Add the stuffed squid tubes, cover the pan and let cook for 15 minutes. If the pan needs a little more liquid, just add some water while cooking.

- Dish out and serve immediately.

no carb sushi roll

Serves 4

Talk about no-carb and fat-free on a sushi roll... And it looks fantastic!
Let this inspire you to be adventurous with sushi.

250 g (9 oz) spinach
4–6 sheets seaweed (nori)
2 Tbsp white sesame seeds

Dipping Sauce

Japanese soy sauce
Sesame oil

- Boil water in a pot and blanch the spinach until it wilts. Drain and set aside.
- Place spinach on some paper towels and squeeze any extra liquid out.
- Place a sheet of seaweed lengthwise on a flat working surface on a bamboo sushi rolling mat.
- Place some spinach across the length of the seaweed sheet. Sprinkle $1/2$ Tbsp sesame seeds on this.
- Using the sushi rolling mat, roll the seaweed and filling away from you into a tight roll. Trim the edges and cut into 4–6 pieces.
- Make dipping sauce. Pour some soy sauce into a small sauce dish. Drizzle some sesame oil over it. Serve as accompaniment to the sushi rolls.

soups

This dish reminds me of one Guy Fawkes Day in London. It was a cold autumn night and I warmed myself up with a huge saucepan of Heinz tomato soup… I love the memory, so here is my healthy option.

tomato soup

Serves 8

Extra virgin olive oil for frying

1 medium onion, peeled and finely chopped

4 cans of chopped tomatoes, each 400 g (14$^{1}/_{3}$ oz)

4 cloves garlic, peeled and crushed

1 Tbsp dried basil

625 ml (20 fl oz / 2$^{1}/_{2}$ cups) vegetable stock (page 136)

French bread, sliced and toasted

- In a large pan, heat a little extra virgin olive oil. Add the onion and sauté for 2 minutes.

- Add the tomatoes and turn the heat down, then add the garlic, basil and stock and simmer for 10 minutes.

- Place in a blender and process till smooth. Serve with a toasted slice of French bread.

noodle soup

Serves 4

There are times when I have arrived in Hong Kong jet lagged and in need of food. I usually call for room service and order a bowl of wonton noodle soup. This recipe reminds me of the comfort I can get from a bowl of warm noodle soup. It hits the spot every time.

150 ml (5 fl oz) chicken stock (page 136,
  or use water and a stock cube)

450 g (1 lb) egg noodles

12 mushrooms, sliced

1 Tbsp sesame oil

1 Tbsp light soy sauce

1 clove garlic, peeled and crushed

6 tiger prawns, peeled

- In a small pot, heat the chicken stock until simmering.
- Add all the remaining ingredients and cook for 4–5 minutes, until the prawns turn pink and are cooked. Remove from the heat and serve.

udon noodles in broth

Serves 4

Udon noodles are my latest craving. They are healthy and so filling and yet I cannot seem to get enough.

700 g (1½ lb) udon noodles

500 ml (16 fl oz / 2 cups) vegetable stock (page 136)

250 g (9 oz) tofu, cubed

1 Tbsp light soy sauce

4 spring onions (scallions), chopped

- Boil the noodles in water for a few minutes and drain.

- Heat the stock and add the noodles, tofu, soy sauce and spring onions.

- Cook for 2–3 minutes and serve.

prawn ball soup

Serves 4 to 6

I love Thailand and all the ingenious food that comes from there. After shooting for the hot US travel show *Bizarre Foods* last December, in Bangkok, I stumbled across fish ball soup. The only thing I did not love was the fatty fish balls. So here is my healthy take on it.

2 eggs

450 g (1 lb) peeled prawns

1 tsp light soy sauce

1.25 litres (40 fl oz / 5 cups) fish stock
  (page 137, or use water and stock cubes)

3 lime leaves

1 stalk lemon grass, hard outer leaves
  removed, ends trimmed, chopped

1 tsp grated ginger

1 clove garlic, peeled and crushed

1 tsp fish sauce

2 red chillies, chopped

A handful of coriander leaves (cilantro)

- In a blender, process the eggs, prawns and soy sauce into
  a paste. Set aside.

- In a large stockpot, heat the stock. Add lime leaves, lemon grass,
  ginger, garlic, fish sauce and chilli. Boil for about 10 minutes.

- Using clean hands, shape the prawn mix into small balls about
  2.5-cm (1-in) in diameter and drop them into the boiling soup.
  Leave to cook for about 3–4 minutes

- Dish out and serve hot with chopped coriander.

mexican black bean soup

Serves 4 to 6

After living in the US for almost 6 years, I am starting to learn about new cuisines, Mexican being one of them. On a family trip to Mexico, I discovered that the Mexicans used black beans for many dishes, from breakfast and lunch to dinner. So here is a black bean recipe I was inspired to create.

1 Tbsp extra virgin olive oil

1 large onion, peeled and chopped

4–6 cloves garlic, peeled and crushed

1.25 litres (40 fl oz / 5 cups) vegetable stock
  (page 136, or use water and stock cubes)

425 g (15 oz) canned black beans, drained

1 cup fresh coriander leaves (cilantro), chopped

3 pickled green jalapeño peppers,
  drained and sliced

- Heat a large stockpot. Add the extra virgin olive oil and onion, and fry for 2–3 minutes. Add the garlic, then the stock and black beans. Cover and simmer for 30 minutes until beans are soft.

- To serve, ladle soup and beans into serving bowls. Garnish with coriander and jalapeño peppers.

low fat mushroom soup

Serves 4 to 6

When I first started cooking, I created an amazing cappuccino of mushroom sauce. I made it for my in-laws, Jennifer and Tony, and my mum and dad. I never told them how much fat was in it and that was why I never ate it myself. But since then, I have come up with a better low fat version. And here it is.

450 g (1 lb) potatoes, peeled, cut into
  1.3-cm ($^1/_2$-in) cubes

3 Tbsp extra virgin olive oil

1 large onion, peeled and chopped

1 clove garlic, peeled and crushed

450 g (1 lb) button mushrooms, with stems,
  coarsely chopped

4 Tbsp dry sherry

250 ml (8 fl oz / 1 cup) chicken stock
  (page 136, or use water and stock cubes)

375 ml (12 fl oz / 1$^1/_2$ cups) low fat milk

- Heat a pot of water and boil the potatoes for 25 minutes. Drain and set aside.

- In a large nonstick pan, add the extra virgin olive oil over medium-high heat. Add the onion and garlic, and cook for 2 minutes.

- Add the mushrooms and cook for 3–4 minutes. Add the sherry and cook for a minute and then add the stock and simmer for 10 minutes.

- In a blender, place the boiled potatoes, milk and everything from the pan and process until smooth.

- Reheat if desired and serve immediately.

edamame soup with tofu

Serves 4

These are ingredients I eat all the time. It is
flavourful and satisfying, and best of all, low in fat.

3 Tbsp extra virgin olive oil

1 large onion, peeled and chopped

2 cloves garlic, peeled and crushed

625 ml (20 fl oz / 2^1/$_2$ cups) chicken stock
  (page 136, or use water and stock cubes)

1 cup edamame beans, out of the pod

1 cup cubed medium tofu

2 cups spinach

1 tsp sesame oil

1 tsp light soy sauce

- In a large saucepan, heat extra virgin olive oil over medium-high heat.
  Cook the onion in the pan for 3–4 minutes.

- Add the garlic and then the stock. Simmer for 10 minutes.

- Add all the remaining ingredients and heat through. Serve hot.

salads

Rice salads develop flavour when they are kept in the refrigerator. Prepare ahead and keep chilled until needed.

asian rice salad

Serves 4

2 cups jasmine rice
2 Tbsp fresh mint leaves, chopped
2 Tbsp fresh basil leaves, chopped
1 cup cooked shredded chicken (no skin)
1 Tbsp sesame oil
1 Tbsp light soy sauce
1 cup cucumber slices
2 Tbsp Chinese rice vinegar
1 Tbsp pine nuts

- Cook the rice as per instructions on pack. Set aside in a large mixing bowl to cool.

- When rice is cool, add all the remaining ingredients, except the pine nuts and mix well.

- In a nonstick pan, toast the pine nuts without using oil. Watch them as they can burn easily. Remove when toasted golden. Top over the rice and refrigerate for 2–3 hours until cold. Serve cold.

asian orange salad

Serves 4

I draw my inspiration from eating at restaurants or from other chefs, and this recipe is one I created after reading *My China* by Kylie Kwong.

4 oranges

1 cup pomegranate seeds

1 cup coriander leaves (cilantro), chopped

1 tsp extra virgin olive oil

- Peel the oranges and cut into 2.5-cm (1-in) slices.
- Place in a bowl with all the other ingredients.
- Mix well and serve.

potato salad

Serves 4

I developed this recipe for my buddy Layne when he asked for a low fat
potato salad.

900 g (2 lb) baby potatoes, sliced in half
4 Tbsp extra virgin olive oil
2 Tbsp Dijon mustard
A handful of chives, finely chopped

- Boil a pot of water and cook the potatoes for
  20–25 minutes. Remove and drain.
- Whisk the extra virgin olive oil and Dijon mustard
  until it resembles mayonnaise. Add the chives.
- Toss the potatoes with the sauce and serve.

arugula salad

I went to Verona with my dad years ago on business and he brought me to one of the best restaurants I have ever eaten at. The experience opened my eyes to fine food. Thanks, Dad, for taking me on trips with you.

4 squid tubes

800 g (1³/₄ lb) arugula (rocket) leaves

Juice of 1 lemon

¹/₂ red onion, peeled and finely sliced

4 Tbsp extra virgin olive oil (use a good one)

1 tsp rock salt

- Slice the squid into rings (0.5-cm or ¹/₄-in slices), then set on paper towels to absorb any liquid.

- Heat a large nonstick pan with a little extra virgin olive oil. Get it really hot, then add the squid and cook for 3–4 minutes. Remove from heat and leave to cool.

- In a large bowl, mix the arugula, lemon juice, onion and extra virgin olive oil.

- Add the cooled squid and mix. Toss in the rock salt and serve.

italian seafood salad

Serves 2 to 4

It does not get better than this classic, naturally healthy and flavourful salad dish. I could eat this all day long. It was at a train station in Milan where I first had this outrageous seafood salad from a little café. It is true that the Italians are passionate about food!

225 g (8 oz) sea scallops

110 g (4 oz) medium prawns

225 g (4 oz) fresh mussels

110 g (4 oz) squid rings

$^1/_2$ cup pitted kalamata olives

2 Tbsp lemon juice

85 ml ($2^1/_2$ fl oz / $^1/_3$ cup)
   extra virgin olive oil

1 large clove garlic, peeled and minced

1 Tbsp fresh parsley, minced

1 Tbsp fresh chives, minced

$^1/_4$ tsp red chilli flakes

6 cups mixed salad greens

1 lemon, sliced

1 medium red onion, peeled and thinly sliced

Sea salt

Freshly ground black pepper

- Bring a large pot of water to boil and place the scallops, prawns, mussels and squid in the boiling water to cook for 2 minutes. Drain. Peel the prawns, and shell the scallops and mussels.

- Place cooked seafood and olives in a large bowl, and toss with lemon juice, extra virgin olive oil, garlic, parsley, chives and red chilli flakes. Chill for 1 hour.

- Divide salad greens among 2 to 4 plates or salad bowls. Spoon seafood over salad greens and garnish with slices of lemon and red onion. Season with salt and freshly ground black pepper.

edamame salad

Serves 4

Edamame are full of protein and goodness. These young
soy beans are brilliant in a salad.

1 tsp wasabi paste

2 Tbsp sesame oil

2 tsp light soy sauce

1 tsp brown sugar

2 Tbsp extra virgin olive oil

Juice of 1 lemon

800 g (1¾ lb) fresh salad leaves
   (a general mix is great)

1 cup edamame beans, out of the pod

½ red onion, finely sliced

- In a bowl, mix the wasabi paste, sesame oil, soy sauce, brown
  sugar, extra virgin olive oil and lemon juice. Set aside dressing.

- In a large salad bowl, mix the salad leaves, edamame beans,
  onion slices and dressing. Toss and serve.

feta cheese & watermelon salad

Serves 2 to 4

This salad has a fantastic colour, tastes so very fresh, and it takes just a few minutes to make. The combination really works well: the sweetness of the watermelon contrasting with the sharpness from the feta cheese.

450 g (1 lb) red seedless watermelon, chilled

2 Tbsp fresh mint leaves

2 Tbsp fresh basil leaves

2 Tbsp extra virgin olive oil

1 cup fat-free feta cheese, crumbled

- Cut the watermelon into chunks and place in a bowl.
- Add the herbs and extra virgin olive oil along with the fat-free feta cheese and toss.
- Serve immediately.

octopus salad

Serves 4

You see this on sushi counters all over the world—it's an option I always take, as it is both low carb and low fat.

500 g (1 lb 1½ oz) baby octopus

2 Tbsp extra virgin olive oil

1 Tbsp light soy sauce

1 Tbsp vinegar

1 tsp sugar

½ cup mixed Japanese pickles, sliced

1 pinch chilli powder

1 Tbsp pickled or fresh ginger, sliced

1 tsp white sesame seeds

- Boil a pot of water and poach the octopus for 3–4 minutes. Drain.

- In a small saucepan, heat the oil, soy sauce, vinegar and sugar and simmer for 2–3 minutes.

- Add the remaining ingredients and mix well. Take off the heat and serve.

mains

Skinny Fish & Chips 77

Chilli 78

Turkey Burgers 80

Mediterranean Beef on Couscous 82

Spicy Tuna on Beans 84

Spaghetti in Tomato Sauce 86

Salmon topped with Strawberries 88

Salmon on Soba Noodles 90

Spicy Miso Sea Bass 92

Mahi Mahi Swordfish 94

Slow Cooked Beef Stew 96

Buffalo Chicken Strips 98

No Cheese Pesto Pasta 100

Mum's Pan-fried Chicken 102

Spaghetti Bolognese 104

I come from England where fish and chips is a staple food. Here is my twist on this all-time favourite, a skinny version. Serve with mushy peas, the classic way.

skinny fish & chips

Serves 4

1 cup bread crumbs (store bought or process day-old bread in a blender)

2 Tbsp fresh dill

2 cloves garlic, peeled

2 eggs

1 Tbsp extra virgin olive oil + more for cooking

4 fish fillets with no skin (I love Dover sole or cod with this)

1 Tbsp fresh mint

1 can drained peas

- Place the bread crumbs, dill and garlic in a blender and process till fine. Set aside on a plate.

- Beat the eggs in a bowl. Dip each fillet of fish in the egg, then coat with bread crumbs.

- Heat a large nonstick pan with a little extra virgin olive oil and fry fillets about 2 minutes each side.

- Process in a blender the mint, peas and extra virgin olive oil into a chunky mix. Serve the fish with the pea mixture.

chilli

Serves 2 to 4

Living in the US, chilli is a staple food. There are many competitions on who has the best recipe. I am not sure if mine is the best (you can be the judge of that) but it could be the healthiest.

Extra virgin olive oil

1 medium onion, peeled and chopped

450 g (1 lb) minced lean beef

1 red chilli, chopped

1 clove garlic, peeled and crushed

1 dash Tabasco sauce

$^1/_2$ cup tomato sauce

4 Tbsp sundried tomato paste

400 g (14$^1/_2$ oz) can chopped tomatoes

425 g (15 oz) can kidney beans

- Heat a little extra virgin olive oil in a nonstick pan. Cook the onion for a minute.

- Add the minced beef and cook for 2–3 minutes.

- Add all the remaining ingredients and simmer for 15 minutes. Dish out and serve.

turkey burgers

Serves 4 to 6

If you use lean turkey mince, they can be almost fat-free.
This is home cooking that's great indoors or on the grill.

900 g (2 lb) lean turkey mince

2 cloves garlic, peeled and crushed

1 Tbsp light soy sauce

1 egg

1 dash Tabasco sauce

2 Tbsp sundried tomato paste

1 Tbsp Djion mustard

1 Tbsp tomato sauce

Extra virgin olive oil

- Combine all ingredients in a bowl. Using clean hands, mix ingredients well together.

- Shape mixture into patties.

- Heat a nonstick pan, heat over a medium heat and add a little extra virgin olive oil. Cook each patty for 2–3 minutes on each side, then repeat until patties are cooked through.

- Serve patties in a burger bun with a garden salad on the side.

mediterranean beef on couscous

Serves 2

I made this on my TV show *Kitchen Takeover*, where I visit the homes of viewers and cook using whatever they have in the kitchen.

3 cups couscous

1 large steak, about 700 g (1$^1/_2$ lb)

4 Tbsp extra virgin olive oil

1 Tbsp Dijon mustard

2 Tbsp balsamic vinegar

$^1/_2$ clove garlic, peeled and crushed

Juice of $^1/_2$ lemon

Fresh thyme, chopped

- Place the couscous in a bowl and cover with boiling water to cover. Cover with a lid and leave for 5 minutes.

- Heat a little oil in a nonstick pan and sear the steak on each side for 3–4 minutes. Remove from heat.

- Combine all remaining ingredients and mix into a dressing. Pour half the dressing over the couscous and mix in well.

- Slice the beef and serve with couscous. Drizzle the remaining dressing over.

spicy tuna on beans

Serves 4

I enjoy eating tuna, so I am always looking for new and delicious ways to serve it. Here, I use hot sesame oil, which can be found in the Japanese section of many supermarkets. I also use it in the California Tuna Spicy Roll (page 112), where a little goes a long way.

500 g (1 lb 1^1/$_2$ oz) green beans

4 tuna steaks each about 180 g (6^1/$_2$ oz)

2 Tbsp sesame oil

2 cloves garlic, peeled and crushed

1 Tbsp mirin

2 red bird's eye chillies, chopped very fine

1 Tbsp light soy sauce

1 Tbsp brown sugar

1 Tbsp hot sesame oil (sesame oil infused with chilli)

- Heat two nonstick pans. In one pan, add a little extra virgin olive oil and wok fry the beans for 3 minutes.

- In the other pan, heat a drizzle of extra virgin olive oil over high heat and sear the tuna steaks for 2 minutes on each side (less if you prefer it very rare). Remove from heat and set aside.

- Add the sesame oil, garlic, mirin, chillies, soy sauce and brown sugar to the beans and let it sizzle and caramelise. Dish out.

- Serve the tuna over the beans and drizzle with the hot sesame oil.

spaghetti in tomato sauce

Serves 4

This is spaghetti you would have in Milan—with just enough sauce to coat the noodles.

450 g (1 lb) spaghetti

1 cup pine nuts

1 Tbsp extra virgin olive oil

1–2 cloves garlic, crushed

2 Tbsp sundried tomato paste

12 pitted black olives, cut in half

A handful of fresh basil leaves, chopped

- Cook the spaghetti following instructions on the pack. Drain and set aside.

- Heat a large nonstick pan and toast the pine nuts without oil. Keep tossing the nuts until they are brown and toasty. Set aside.

- Reheat the pan and add the extra virgin olive oil and garlic. Cook for 30 seconds to a minute.

- Add the spaghetti, pine nuts, sundried tomato paste and the olives, and toss for a minute or so in the pan to reheat the noodles. Serve immediately with some fresh basil.

salmon topped with strawberries

Serves 2

I conduct many cooking classes and the participants are usually women, so I was surprised to see a teenage boy in one of these classes I was conducting at the Mandarin Oriental Hong Kong. Max has a passion for cooking and now has a summer job at Zuma in Hong Kong, an upmarket restaurant serving contemporary Japanese cuisine. This recipe is from Max.

2 salmon fillets

800 g (1³/₄ lb) baby potatoes, peeled

Fine sea salt

Ground black pepper

Extra virgin olive oil

2 carrots, about 285 g (10 oz)

250 ml (8 fl oz / 1 cup) orange juice

A handful of fresh basil leaves

15 g (¹/₂ oz) fresh Parmesan cheese, grated finely

2 strawberries, hulled

Marinade

¹/₄ tsp fine sea salt

¹/₄ tsp black pepper

2 tsp extra virgin olive oil

Juice of ¹/₂ lemon

- Preheat the oven to 220°C (440°F).

- Marinate the salmon fillets, with salt, pepper, extra virgin olive oil and lemon juice.

- Boil the potatoes until soft, then drain and mash into a paste. Season with salt, pepper and extra virgin olive oil. Mix well and cover to keep hot.

- Slice carrots and place into a sauté pan. Add extra virgin olive oil and sauté carrots for about 3 minutes. Add orange juice and make sure the carrots are spread out so they absorb the juice evenly. Cook until the carrots are tender, and the juice is reduced into a sauce.

- Put salmon fillets in oven and grill for 10 minutes. Salmon should be golden on the outside and pink inside.

- Cut basil leaves very finely and put into a mixing bowl, add extra virgin olive oil and finely grated Parmesan. Add pesto to mashed potato and mix well.

- Arrange the salmon on a serving plate with the strawberries and serve with the carrots and mashed potato on the side.

salmon on soba noodles

Serves 4

This dish is perfect and I just can't stop making it. Try it for yourself!

4 skinless salmon fillets, each about 150 g (5$^1/_3$ oz)

1 tsp brown sugar

2 Tbsp sesame oil

700 g (1$^1/_2$ lb) fresh soba noodles

1 tsp hot sesame oil (sesame oil infused with chilli)

2 shallots, peeled and finely chopped

4 spring onions (scallions), chopped

1 Tbsp light soy sauce

500 g (1 lb 1$^1/_2$ oz) spinach

- Place the salmon on a baking tray. Sprinkle with brown sugar and 1 Tbsp sesame oil. Place under the grill or broiler and cook for 6–7 minutes until brown.

- Boil a pot of water and cook the soba noodles for 4–5 minutes. Drain and place in a mixing bowl with the remaining sesame oil.

- Reheat the water and blanch the spinach for a minute, until wilted. Drain.

- Combine hot sesame oil, shallots, spring onions and soy sauce in a bowl and mix well. Toss the soba noodles.

- Serve the noodles, with spinach and salmon and drizzle over any remaining sauce.

spicy miso sea bass

Serves 4

There are over 12 kinds of sea bass. For this recipe, use Chilean sea bass or black cod as it is thicker and tastes fantastic. I first tried this at a restaurant in Santa Monica and raced home immediately after dinner to try making my own version of it.

2 Tbsp miso paste

2 cloves garlic, peeled and crushed

2 tsp sesame oil

1 Tbsp honey

2 Tbsp mirin

4 sea bass fillets, each about 150 g (5$^1/_3$ oz)

2 Tbsp hot Buffalo wing sauce

Cooked jasmine rice

- Mix the miso paste, garlic, sesame oil, honey and mirin. Brush over the sea bass fillets and place on a baking tray.

- Place under the grill or broiler for 6–8 minutes until the top has browned.

- Mix the remaining sauce with the hot Buffalo wing sauce and heat it till it comes to the boil.

- Serve the sea bass with rice and drizzle the sauce over.

mahi mahi swordfish

Serves 4

Growing up, we used to go to the Florida Keys. My brother is a fantastic fisherman so we used to go out on the boat with my dad and catch these brilliant fish. That was, until I got bored and pretended to be sea-sick to make them come on shore. Sorry Jonny, for being such a brat. So this recipe is for Jonny.

600 g (1 lb 5$^1/_3$ oz) broccoli

4 mahi mahi fillets (no skin) each about 300 g (11 oz)

4 tsp Cajun spice (available from supermarkets)

1 lemon, quartered

- Steam the broccoli for just 3–4 minutes, being careful not to overcook it. Drain and set aside.

- Preheat the oven to 230°C (450°F). Place the mahi mahi on a baking tray and top with Cajun spice.

- Cook for 12–15 minutes and serve with the broccoli. Garnish with lemon quarters.

slow cooked beef stew

Serves 6

I recommend doubling the quantities on this as it gets better and better with keeping and reheating. I will probably add this to my creations for the KLM inflight menu as not many dishes can stand up to being reheated like this one!

1 Tbsp extra virgin olive oil

1.4 kg (3 lb) lean beef cubes

1 onion, peeled and diced

50 ml (1$^2/_3$ fl oz) red wine

1 tsp plain (all-purpose) flour

12 baby carrots

12 baby potatoes, halved

12 brussel sprouts

3 cloves garlic, peeled and crushed

50 ml (1$^2/_3$ fl oz) beef stock (using stock cubes and
  water, prepared according to instructions)

- Heat a large stockpot that has a cover and retains heat well. Add the extra virgin olive oil and fry the beef cubes for 3–4 minutes until browned on all sides.

- Add the onion and fry for a few minutes. Add the red wine and lower heat to a simmer. Whisk the flour into the stock, then add it and everything else to the pot. Cover and simmer over very low heat for 40 minutes until beef is very tender.

- Serve hot.

buffalo chicken strips

Serves 4

Ok, so I have bad days too, and they consist of pizza and Buffalo wings. I do this when I arrive home from a long trip, jet-lagged, tired and wanting a treat. Buffalo wings are deep-fried, but here's my Twist on it after many, many attempts.

Extra virgin olive oil
900 g (2 lb) chicken breast strips
  (no skin)
250 ml (8 fl oz / 1 cup) chilli sauce
4 celery stalks, cut into sticks
2 Tbsp fat-free mayonnaise

- Heat a large pan with a drizzle of extra virgin olive oil.

- Sear the chicken on each side for about 4 minutes, until cooked all the way through. Remove from the heat and add half the chilli sauce. Make sure the sauce coats the chicken well.

- Remove chicken from the pan and place onto a serving dish. Add the remaining sauce.

- Serve the Buffalo chicken strips with sliced celery sticks and fat-free mayonnaise on the side.

no cheese pesto pasta

Serves 4

Pasta dishes are generally rather healthy except for the added fat from cheese. This recipe is made without cheese and flavoured with a fresh pesto made only with basil and pine nuts.

$^1/_2$ cup fresh basil leaves

$^1/_2$ cup pine nuts

1 clove garlic, peeled

3 Tbsp extra virgin olive oil

450 g (1 lb) pasta, choose tube-shaped ones like penne or macaroni

- In a blender, process the basil, pine nuts, garlic and extra virgin olive oil together.

- Cook the pasta following instructions on the pack. Drain and set aside.

- Heat a large saucepan. Add the pasta and basil pesto and mix well, cooking for about 1 minute.

- Dish out and serve immediately.

mum's pan-fried chicken

Serves 4

My mum used to cook dinner every night for us, always preparing it with fresh, ingredients and making it with love. I asked her for this recipe which I grew up eating, during the period when I started to develop a love for cooking. Thanks to the best mum in the world!

1 Tbsp plain (all-purpose) flour

Salt

Ground pepper to taste

4 skinless and boneless chicken fillets,
  cut into bite-size pieces

1 Tbsp extra virgin olive oil

1 red capsicum, diced

1/2 onion, peeled and chopped

1 clove garlic, peeled and crushed

6 cherry tomatoes, sliced

2 large carrots, chopped

6 mushrooms, sliced

1 small can of peas and any other
  vegetables you wish to use

125 ml (4 fl oz / 1/2 cup) water

- Put the flour in a plastic bag and add salt, pepper and chicken shaking it around until chicken is well-coated.

- Heat extra virgin olive oil in a wok and add the chicken. Stir-fry until almost cooked. Remove the chicken to a plate.

- Reheat the wok and add the capsicum, onion, garlic, tomatoes, carrots, mushrooms, peas and stir-fry for a few minutes to mix well.

- Add water and allow to boil.

- Return chicken to the wok and stir-fry until chicken is cooked through. Season with salt and pepper.

- Dish out and serve immediately.

spaghetti bolognese

Serves 4 to 6

Spaghetti bolognese is wholesome and hearty, and it is my wife, Jane's favourite comfort food.

450 g (1 lb) spaghetti
1 Tbsp extra virgin olive oil
1 onion, finely chopped
450 g (1 lb) minced beef, low-fat
250 ml (8 fl oz / 1 cup) tomato sauce
400 g (14^1/$_3$ oz) can chopped tomatoes
4 cloves garlic, peeled and crushed

- Cook the spaghetti following instructions on the pack. Drain and set aside.

- Heat a nonstick pan and add the extra virgin olive oil. Cook the onion for 2 minutes, add the beef and stir as you cook for a few minutes.

- Add the tomato sauce, can of tomatoes and garlic, and simmer for 8 minutes.

- Add spaghetti to the sauce, mix well to coat the noodles and heat through.

- Garnish as desired and serve immediately.

snacks

I drew my inspiration for this dish from the Chinese egg fried rice. My dish is flavoured with mirin and miso paste, two ingredients I enjoy using in my cooking. This dish is a favourite with my daughter.

japanese fried rice

Serves 4

150 g (5$^1/_3$ oz) rice (jasmine is great)

Extra virgin olive oil for frying

$^1/_2$ white onion, peeled and chopped finely

1 cup shiitake mushrooms, chopped

1 carrot, peeled and finely chopped

$^1/_2$ cup frozen green peas

1 Tbsp mirin

1 Tbsp miso paste

- Cook the rice following instructions on the pack. Set aside to cool. You should end up with 450 g (1 lb) of cooked rice.

- In a large pan, heat some extra virgin olive oil. Add the onion and cook for a minute. Add the mushrooms and carrot and cook for another 3–4 minutes. Add the peas, then the mirin and stir-fry for 30 seconds. Remove from heat.

- Mix in the miso paste and then add the cooled rice and mix well.

- Dish out and serve.

eggs & chips

Serves 4

This was one of my childhood favourites. I love dipping the chips into the soft egg yolks. It was what I liked to have for tea (otherwise known as dinner). My Twist to this dish is the low fat chips or fries.

4–6 potatoes, peeled

12 eggs

4 Tbsp extra virgin olive oil

2 tsp rock salt

- Preheat oven to 230°C (450°F).

- Slice the potatoes into chips or fries and throw them in a mixing bowl with the extra virgin olive oil. Coat well. Arrange the chips or fries in a single layer on a baking tray.

- Roast for 20 minutes in the oven, then toss the chips or fries around and return to the oven for another 12–16 minutes or until golden brown.

- Heat a small nonstick pan and cook the eggs over medium heat individually or 3 at a time until eggs are just cooked and yolks still soft.

- Serve the chips or fries with the eggs and a garden salad, if desired.

veggie wrap

Serves 4

Beans are a great way to stop curb your craving for carbs as they are so filling and satisfying. They are my comfort food. Add these to a wrap and it makes a brilliant meal!

450 g (1 lb) can black beans, drained

2 Tbsp vegetable stock (page 136, or use water and vegetable stock cubes)

1 clove garlic, peeled

4 low fat, low carb wraps

A handful of arugula (rocket) leaves

- In a blender, process the beans, stock and garlic into a thick paste.

- Spoon a quarter of the paste onto a wrap and top with arugula. Roll the wrap up. Repeat with the remaining ingredients.

- Slice and serve.

california spicy tuna roll

Serves 2 to 4

I have tried to make sushi as easy to prepare as possible. This is a spicy fish version of the No Carb Sushi Roll (page 44). This spicy tuna roll is on the menu in some of the best Japanese restaurants in the world.

2 cups sushi rice

500 ml (16 fl oz / 2 cups) water

2 Tbsp rice vinegar

220 g (8 oz) sashimi grade tuna

1 shallot, peeled and finely chopped

2 tsp hot sesame oil (sesame oil
  infused with chilli)

1 Tbsp low fat mayonnaise

4 sheets seaweed (nori)

Japanese soy sauce

Wasabi

- In a rice cooker or covered saucepan, boil the rice and water for 20 minutes. When done, fluff the rice up and transfer to a large mixing bowl. Add the rice vinegar and mix in. Set aside.

- Chop the tuna well and mix in a bowl with the shallot, hot sesame oil and mayonnaise.

- Place a seaweed sheet on bamboo sushi rolling mat. Spread some rice in a thin layer three quarters way up the sheet. Spoon some tuna mix lengthways on in a line on the edge of the rice nearest to you, then roll up tightly, away from you. Repeat with remaining ingredients.

- Trim off the edges, then cut each roll into 4. Serve with some soy sauce and wasabi, if desired.

roasted butternut squash

Serves 4

Feel like you want to binge on carbs? Then try this dish which will satisfy your craving, but yet is low on carbs and fat! My mum taught me this one, and I added the garlic.

2 butternut squash

2–3 Tbsp extra virgin olive oil

1 bulb garlic, cut in half horizontally

2 tsp rock salt

* Preheat the oven to 230°C (450°F)

* Peel the butternut squash and slice in half. Take out the seeds and discard. Place the butternut squash on a baking tray. Drizzle over with extra virgin olive oil.

* Place the bulb of garlic on a sheet of aluminium foil. Drizzle the two halves with 1 Tbsp extra virgin olive oil, place the halves together and wrap with foil. Place on the baking tray with the butternut squash.

* Roast for 40–50 minutes. Unwrap the bulb of garlic, being careful not to scorch your fingers. Squeeze out the meat from each clove of garlic which has been baked to a soft consistency. Sprinkle rock salt on garlic and butternut squash. Serve immediately.

wasabi pea mash

Serves 4

I love this version that not only has the comfort of mashed
potatoes, but the crunch of wasabi peas as well.

4–6 large baking potatoes, peeled and quartered

125 ml (4 fl oz / $^1/_2$ cup) skim milk

1 cup wasabi peas

Salt to taste

Ground black pepper to taste

- Boil a large pot of water and cook the potatoes
  for 35 minutes. Drain.
- Using an electric whisk, whip the potatoes while
  slowly adding the skim milk, blending until smooth.
- Add the wasabi peas and season with salt and
  pepper. Serve.

bruschetta

Serves 4 to 8, normally served as a starter

This is an Italian classic—and there are so many variations on this dish.
I make it a lot as it is one of my wife's favourites and it is quick and easy
for serving at dinner parties. Just don't put the topping on the bread too
early, as it makes the bread go soggy. About 20 minutes before is fine.

1 small red onion, peeled and finely chopped

A handful of fresh basil leaves, shredded

8 medium tomatoes, seeded and chopped

1 clove garlic, peeled and crushed

Juice of $1/2$ lemon

2 Tbsp extra virgin olive oil

1 small red chilli, chopped very finely

220 g (8 oz) fat-free feta cheese, crumbled

1 French bread loaf, cut into 2.5-cm (1-in) slices
and toasted

- Place all the ingredients, except the bread, in a bowl
  and mix well.
- Top a spoonful on each slice of toasted French bread
  and serve.

prawns with green beans

Serves 4

This is a nice mix of protein and some carbs. Try this with
canned tuna too!

450 g (1 lb) prawns, peeled and deveined
300 g (11 oz) green beans
$^1/_4$ red onion, peeled and finely sliced

Dressing

1 Tbsp chopped capers
2 Tbsp extra virgin olive oil
Juice of $^1/_2$ lemon
1 tsp Dijon mustard
A handful of fresh basil leaves, chopped

- Boil a pot of water and poach prawns in it for
  3–5 minutes or until prawns turn pink. Remove
  prawns, drain and set aside.

- Boil another pot of water and add the green
  beans. Cook for 6 minutes. Drain and place in
  a mixing bowl. Add the prawns and onion.

- Mix the dressing ingredients in another bowl,
  then add to the bean and prawn mixture. Toss
  well and serve.

Something Sweet

Bananas are a great way to add natural sweetness to baked treats. I love this as a dessert.

banana cake

Serves 4

200 g (7 oz / 2 cups) plain (all-purpose) flour

1 tsp baking powder

$^3/_4$ tsp baking soda

$^1/_4$ tsp salt

150 g (5$^1/_3$ oz / $^3/_4$ cup) brown sugar

1 egg, lightly beaten

4 Tbsp vegetable or peanut oil

125 ml (4 fl oz / $^1/_2$ cup) nonfat milk

3 medium-size ripe bananas, peeled and mashed

1 tsp vanilla extract

- Preheat the oven to 200°C (400°F).

- Grease a 23–25 cm (9–10-in) cake pan using a cooking spray.

- Mix the flour, baking powder, baking soda and salt in a bowl.

- Place the brown sugar and egg in a large mixing bowl. Beat with a mixer at medium speed until fluffy. Add the oil, milk, mashed bananas and vanilla extract and mix until well blended.

- Gradually mix in flour mixture until incorporated into a thick batter.

- Pour batter into prepared cake pan and bake for 30 minutes.

- Test that cake is done by inserting a cake tester or skewer into the centre of cake. It should come out clean.

cocoa banana soufflé

Serves 4 to 6

Don't be put off by the idea of making a soufflé. This is simple and foolproof.

2 ripe bananas
1 tsp vanilla paste (or extract)
2 tsp corn flour (cornstarch)
1/4 cup cocoa powder
2 egg whites
2 Tbsp sugar

- Preheat oven to 200°C (400°F). Grease 4 to 6 ramekins with a little oil.

- Mash bananas with vanilla.

- Sift corn flour and cocoa powder and mix well.

- Beat egg whites with sugar until soft peaks form.

- Fold a quarter of egg whites into banana mixture. When incorporated, fold in the rest of the egg whites. Spoon mixture into ramekins. Bake for 15 minutes.

- The soufflés will deflate a little when removed from the oven, but that's normal. Serve immediately.

meringues with almonds & chocolate rice

Serves 4

My mum used to make these often. They were sticky and soft on the inside and crumbly on the outside. She used to make a cream cake for entertaining with layers of cream and meringues with fresh strawberries. When the guests left, I used to pile through the meringue part.

4 egg whites

$^1/_4$ tsp salt

225 g (8 oz / 1$^1/_4$ cups) castor sugar

$^1/_2$ tsp vanilla extract

Chocolate rice

Chopped almonds

- Preheat oven to 110°C (225°F).

- Beat egg whites and salt until soft peaks form. Add half the sugar and continue beating until stiff peaks form. Fold in the rest of the sugar and vanilla.

- Spoon mixture into a piping bag fitted with a star nozzle and pipe mounds on a greased baking tray, spacing them about 2.5-cm (1-in) apart. Bake for 2 hours.

- Sprinkle with some chocolate rice and chopped almonds Serve.

frozen yoghurt

Serves 4

This is so quick and easy to make. My 8-year-old daughter can also do this but without the blender. She just mashes it all together.

4 cups frozen strawberries
110 g (4 oz / $\frac{1}{2}$ cup) sugar
2 cups nonfat plain yoghurt

- Place all the ingredients in a blender and process until fine.
- Pour mixture into a freezer container and leave for 6 hours to set. Serve chilled.

grilled pineapple

Serves 4 to 6

There is such a natural flavour to pineapple... and when it is grilled it takes on a lovely melting texture. This needs nothing else and it reminds me of my time in Hawaii where I had the best pineapple ever.

1 pineapple, peeled and cut into wedges or slices
  (you can substitute with canned pineapple rings,
  but cut down on the brown sugar as the pineapples
  are already soaked in syrup)
4 Tbsp brown sugar
Juice of 1 lemon
1 Tbsp honey
2 cups ricotta cheese
$1/2$ tsp vanilla extract
110 g (4 oz / $1/2$ cup) sugar

- Lay the pineapple out on a baking tray. Sprinkle with the sugar and the lemon juice.

- Drizzle with honey and place under the grill for 4–5 minutes or until it caramelises.

- Mix the ricotta cheese with the vanilla and sugar.

- Serve the pineapple with the ricotta cheese mix.

pumpkin pie

Serves 6 to 8

Surprisingly, this can be very low in fat if you use low fat milk in place of cream. I made this with a great chef, Chef Patrick in Minneapolis, for my TV show, *Kitchen Takeover*. It was a wonderful experience and I am grateful that he taught me how to make desserts.

450 g (1 lb) brown sugar

2 pinches of salt

Pinch of black pepper

Pinch of ground ginger

Pinch of ground mace

Pinch of ground nutmeg

4 eggs

1 Tbsp vanilla extract

700 g (1½ lb) pumpkin purée,
  canned or fresh

265 ml (9 fl oz) low-fat milk

150 ml (5 fl oz) milk

1 pie shell, 23–28-cm (9–11in) pie
  shell, store bought

- Preheat oven to 190°C (365°F).

- Add all dry ingredients in a bowl and mix together, making sure there are no lumps.

- Add eggs to dry mix and mix well. Add pumpkin and mix together. Add low fat milk and milk, then add vanilla.

- Mix everything together and pour into pie shell. Do not overfill shell. Put pie in oven for 20 minutes. Then lower temperature to 180°C (350°F) for another 15 minutes.

- When done, the middle of the filling should be set, and it should not wobble if the pie is shaken gently from side to side. Bake for another 5–10 minutes if necessary. Remove and let cool.

Daniel Green launches his TV programmes, *Healthy Eating
with Daniel Green* and *World Dining with Daniel Green.*
These two programmes are broadcast over six cities in Asia—Brunei,
Hong Kong, Indonesia, Malaysia, Singapore and Taiwan.

Green's menu planner

*These are my suggestions for a perfect balanced meal.
These recipes work so well together—whether served
for a dinner party or just an everyday family meal.*

Asian Comfort Food

Sticky Spicy Edamame
Noodles in Broth
New Mango Smoothie

Mexican Twist

Scallops Ceviche
Mexican Black Bean Soup
Cocoa Banana Soufflé

Japanese Bliss

Japanese Oysters
Spicy Miso Sea Bass
Frozen Yoghurt

American Twist

California Spicy Tuna Roll
Mahi Mahi Swordfish
Banana Cake

Comfort Food

Buffalo Chicken Strips
Turkey Burgers
Potato Salad

Breakfast Feast

Low Fat Fry-Up
Low Fat Muffins
Berry Blast

Elegant Entertaining

Poor Man's Caviar
Low Fat Mushroom Soup
Spicy Tuna on Beans
Meringues with Almonds &
 Chocolate Rice

Late Night Hunger (options)

Eggs & Chips
Spaghetti in Tomato Sauce
Wasabi Pea Mash

basic recipes

Vegetable Stock

Makes about 625 ml (20 fl oz / 2½ cups)

Making your own stock need not be a chore. This vegetable stock is easy to make and you'll see for yourself the difference in the taste alone.

2 carrots, chopped
2 onions, peeled and quartered
2 celery sticks, chopped
½ fennel bulb, chopped
Stalk from a head of broccoli, chopped
4 large tomatoes
8 button mushrooms, halved
6 black peppercorns
1 bay leaf
4 Tbsp tomato paste
3 parsley stalks
1 litre (32 fl oz / 4 cups) water

- Place all ingredients in a large pot and simmer for about 50 minutes. Strain the stock before use.

Chicken Stock

Makes about 625 ml (20 fl oz / 2½ cups)

The key to a good low-fat chicken stock is to refrigerate it, then skim off the fat from the surface. Homemade stocks can be stored in the refrigerator for 2–3 days and up to a month in the freezer.

1 medium chicken, cut into 8 pieces
6 button mushrooms, halved
½ tsp salt
1 tsp black peppercorns
2 carrots, chopped
2 onions, peeled and quartered
2 celery sticks, chopped
3 cloves garlic
4 large tomatoes
3 parsley stalks
1 litre (32 fl oz / 4 cups) water

- Place all ingredients in a large pot and simmer for about 50 minutes.

- Strain the stock, then leave to cool and refrigerate for about 1 hour.

- Remove the layer of fat from the surface of stock using a large metal spoon.

- Reheat the stock and use as required.

Fish Stock

Makes about 625 ml (20 fl oz / 2¹/₂ cups)

This is another stock that can be prepared without fuss.

6 large tiger prawns

Trimmings (heads, skin and bones) of
  4 medium size fish (sea bass or salmon)

2 carrots, chopped

2 onions, peeled and quartered

2 celery sticks, chopped

3 cloves garlic

4 large tomatoes

4 Tbsp tomato paste

3 parsley stalks

1 litre (32 fl oz / 4 cups) water

- Place all ingredients in a large pot and simmer for about 50 minutes. Strain the stock before use.

"I hope to help people be better able to manage their weight by eating healthily."

Full name   : Daniel Green
Nickname   : Dan
Birthday   : September 1, 1970
Hometown : London

Years as a television host, presenter
& celebrity chef: 1999–present.

Present career: Host at ShopNBC
since 2004. I do every product category
but I specialise in cooking.

Favourite colour: Black. It is so easy and
always looks smart.

Favourite hobbies: Cooking and travelling.

Favourite food: Thai. I love the fresh, clean
flavours of Thai food and I have even written
a cookbook on Thai food!

More About Me

As a child, I really enjoyed… tennis, cooking and being a spoilt younger brother.

How I got into the home shopping business… I hosted cooking and travel shows in the UK and started doing some work in the US. My agent asked me what I thought about shopping TV and I was thrilled at the chance to explore it.

The best part about being a ShopNBC host is… 'live' TV. It changes all the time. Good or bad, it is always so exciting.

My favourite on-air moments are… those funny moments when I just burst out laughing!

My most embarrassing moment on air… Well I said something I shouldn't, but it was funny. I also almost burnt down the house I was doing a 'live' cooking show in, on UK TV.

The most challenging part of hosting is… I enjoy it so much I really can't think of it as being challenging.

Off camera, I… am the same person. You can't perform on 'live' TV. You have to be yourself.

My greatest achievement… is writing my first cookbook. I was quite taken aback when I saw it for the first time. Then on the third page it said "To Eleanor with love." (That's my daughter.) Needless to say I got teary-eyed.

I am known as The Model Cook… because after I lost weight around 18 years ago I went into modeling for a few years. It was fun but not a career I wanted to follow. Then I ended up cooking to lose weight, and here I am!

My food… is not intended for a diet. I simply lower the fat content in the dishes I love to eat. This way, I hope to help people be better able to manage their weight by eating healthily.

I spend my free time… with my wife and daughter as much as possible. I do love to travel too.

In my personal life, I am motivated by… my parents and my family. I just want to bring up my daughter with the same values that my wife and I share.

My mentors are… a brilliant director Stephen Daldry who has great success in his career but possesses such modesty. On a personal level, my wife Jane. She always reminds me of what's real and makes the right choices all the time.

My friends and family would describe me as… someone who does not take himself too seriously, and who is always looking for a way to make people laugh.

My hidden talents are… in fishing. But sadly, I don't get much of a chance to do so nowadays.

The accomplishment I am most proud of… is making my dream to be on TV one day happen.

I always look forward to… spending time with my wife and daughter.

If I wasn't hosting cooking shows, the career path I'd have followed would be… still something in the form of cooking and travel. I've always had a passion for the two.

I am really bad at this, but wish I was great at… singing. I would love to be able to sing, and I am really, really bad. Even the cats leave the room when I sing!

weights & measures

Quantities for this book are given in Metric and American (spoon and cup) measures. Standard spoon and cup measurements used are: 1 teaspoon = 5 ml, 1 tablespoon = 15 ml, 1 cup = 250 ml. All measures are level unless otherwise stated.

Liquid & Volume Measures

Metric	Imperial	American
5 ml	$1/6$ fl oz	1 teaspoon
10 ml	$1/3$ fl oz	1 dessertspoon
15 ml	$1/2$ fl oz	1 tablespoon
60 ml	2 fl oz	$1/4$ cup (4 tablespoons)
85 ml	$2^{1}/2$ fl oz	$1/3$ cup
90 ml	3 fl oz	$3/8$ cup (6 tablespoons)
125 ml	4 fl oz	$1/2$ cup
180 ml	6 fl oz	$3/4$ cup
250 ml	8 fl oz	1 cup
300 ml	10 fl oz ($1/2$ pint)	$1^{1}/4$ cups
375 ml	12 fl oz	$1^{1}/2$ cups
435 ml	14 fl oz	$1^{3}/4$ cups
500 ml	16 fl oz	2 cups
625 ml	20 fl oz (1 pint)	$2^{1}/2$ cups
750 ml	24 fl oz ($1^{1}/5$ pints)	3 cups
1 litre	32 fl oz ($1^{3}/5$ pints)	4 cups
1.25 litres	40 fl oz (2 pints)	5 cups
1.5 litres	48 fl oz ($2^{2}/5$ pints)	6 cups
2.5 litres	80 fl oz (4 pints)	10 cups

Dry Measures

Metric	Imperial
30 grams	1 ounce
45 grams	$1^{1}/2$ ounces
55 grams	2 ounces
70 grams	$2^{1}/2$ ounces
85 grams	3 ounces
100 grams	$3^{1}/2$ ounces
110 grams	4 ounces
125 grams	$4^{1}/2$ ounces
140 grams	5 ounces
280 grams	10 ounces
450 grams	16 ounces (1 pound)
500 grams	1 pound, $1^{1}/2$ ounces
700 grams	$1^{1}/2$ pounds
800 grams	$1^{3}/4$ pounds
1 kilogram	2 pounds, 3 ounces
1.5 kilograms	3 pounds, $4^{1}/2$ ounces
2 kilograms	4 pounds, 6 ounces

Oven Temperature

	°C	°F	Gas Regulo
Very slow	120	250	1
Slow	150	300	2
Moderately slow	160	325	3
Moderate	180	350	4
Moderately hot	190/200	370/400	5/6
Hot	210/220	410/440	6/7
Very hot	230	450	8
Super hot	250/290	475/550	9/10

Length

Metric	Imperial
0.5 cm	$1/4$ inch
1 cm	$1/2$ inch
1.5 cm	$3/4$ inch
2.5 cm	1 inch

index of recipes

International TV Personality, Chef and Author—
Daniel Green, The Model Cook
www.themodelcook.com